Author:
John Malam studied ancient history and
archaeology at the University of Birmingham,
after which he worked as an archaeologist at the
Ironbridge Gorge Museum, Shropshire. He is now
an author, specialising in information books for
children. He lives in Cheshire with his wife and
their two children.

Artist:
David Antram was born in Brighton, England,
in 1958. He studied at Eastbourne College of Art
and then worked in advertising for 15 years before
becoming a full-time artist. He has illustrated
many children's non-fiction books.

Series creator:
David Salariya was born in Dundee,
Scotland. He has illustrated a wide range of books
and has created and designed many new series for
publishers both in the UK and overseas. In 1989
he established The Salariya Book Company. He
lives in Brighton with his wife, the illustrator
Shirley Willis, and their son Jonathan.

Editors:
Karen Barker Smith
Stephanie Cole

Published in Great Britain in 2002 by
Book House, an imprint of
The Salariya Book Company Ltd
Book House, 25 Marlborough Place,
Brighton BN1 1UB

Visit The Salariya Book Company at:
www.salariya.com
www.book-house.co.uk

A catalogue record for this book is available from
the British Library.

ISBN 1 904194 19 2

Printed and bound in Belgium.
Printed on paper from sustainable forests.

Avoid becoming a Pirates' Prisoner!

How did I get into this mess?!

The Danger Zone

Written by
John Malam

Illustrated by
David Antram

Created and designed by
David Salariya

BOOK HOUSE

Contents

Introduction

It is the year 1716 and the Caribbean Sea is the haunt of English pirates. These rogues are the menace of the Spanish Main – the area of land and sea between the northern coast of South America and the southern shores of North America. The pirates like to lie in wait for Spanish treasure ships. They are full of gold and valuables plundered from the peoples of the New World.

You are the captain of one of these ships. You hope to sail home safely to Spain, unseen by the scoundrels that lurk in these dangerous waters. To the pirates, your golden galleon is a great prize and, if they capture it, you wouldn't want to become a pirates' prisoner!

Treasure fleet! Your ship sets sail

In your ship's hold:

GOLD AND RICHES. At the port of Cartagena you collected gold, emeralds, pearls and valuable timber from the rainforests of South America.

VERA CRUZ. At this port you stopped for porcelain, silk and spices from lands across the Pacific Ocean.

SUPPLIES. At Havana you took on board copper, food and water for the long voyage home.

You are the captain of a Spanish galleon. It is a large slow-moving ship armed with cannons and a hold full of precious cargo. Once a year you sail home to Spain from a port in the Spanish Main. It would be foolish to set sail on your own so you sail in convoy with many other galleons, all loaded with the treasures of the New World. There is safety in numbers and if a pirate attacks the fleet he's only likely to pick on one ship at a time. You hope it won't be yours!

SPANISH CAPTAIN. Dressed in your captain's clothes you are a grand sight. Your crew respect you and you are proud that your ship has never been attacked by pirates.

We are shipshape and ready to go!

Handy hint

Sail close to the warship that sails with the fleet – it's to protect you.

NORTH AMERICA

BAHAMAS

Havana

Vera Cruz

CUBA

CENTRAL AMERICA

JAMAICA

Caribbean Sea

HISPANIOLA

N

W

E

S

WEST INDIES

Cartagena

SOUTH AMERICA

THE FLEET. In the 1600s the Spanish treasure fleet sailed with as many as 90 galleons. Now, in the early 1700s, the fleet is smaller, with fewer than 12 ships.

Map of the Spanish Main in the 18th century

Pirates! Wolves of the sea

From privateer to pirate

Privateers were English, French and Dutch men who had permission from their governments to attack Spanish ships and territory in the New World. That has come to an end now, but some privateers are still up to their old tricks and steal for themselves as pirates.

After

Before

Englishnglish pirates have been attacking the Spanish treasure fleet for almost 200 years. Sometimes they raid ships while they are at anchor in port, taking them completely by surprise. Other times they take to the open sea, to look for a ship that has fallen behind the rest of the fleet. The first twenty years of the 18th century have been a good time for piracy in the Spanish Main and now there are more pirates here than ever before. They have turned many island ports into their own safe havens.

NO MORE WAR. England and Holland were at war against France and Spain until 1714. Many sea captains fought as privateers, raiding Spanish ships. The end of the war has put them out of a job, so now they've turned to piracy.

Treasure ships ahoy, Cap'n!

PIRATE HAVEN. New Providence offers safety to pirate ships and their crews. It's a wild, lawless island, where hundreds of pirates are based – a perfect location from which to make a raid on a treasure ship.

9

Pirates' prize! Your ship is attacked

Avast! Here be pirates!

THEIR SHIP. It is a sloop, a small lightweight vessel that cuts quickly through the water – perfect for surprise attacks.

PIRATE FLAG. The Jolly Roger is black with a human skull. It is designed to strike fear into your heart.

CAPTAIN. He's an outlaw who is known for getting exactly what he wants.

Your ship sets sail with six others, all bound for Spain. But your galleon is so weighed down with loot that it can't keep up with the fleet. You fall behind and are on your own with no one to come to your aid if something happens.

A ship has been following the fleet at a distance and now it closes in on you. The ship raises its flag to identify itself – only then do you know you're about to be attacked by pirates! Their smaller, faster ship comes alongside and the English pirates are soon boarding your vessel to relieve you of its treasure.

WEAPONS. They might be dressed in rags, but pirates are armed with a fearsome range of weapons.

Boarding axe

Flintlock pistol

Musket

Cutlass

Captured!

The pirate captain is not satisfied with pinching the loot from your ship. He wants the treasure from the rest of the fleet too. That is why you will come in useful. Now you are the pirates' prisoner, you are at their mercy. They want you to tell them what course the other treasure ships are taking. It's no use saying you don't know, because these ruffians know you do. Be warned – they have ways of making you talk!

So where be your fleet, then?

Rules of piracy

BOOTY. Your cargo of treasure now belongs to the pirates and it will be divided among them. The captain and the quartermaster will get double shares.

COMPENSATION. Pirates look after each other. An injured man will be cared for by his shipmates and he'll receive extra pay if he loses a limb.

Handy hint

Be friendly to the pirate captain. You never know, if he likes you, he might treat you like a fellow captain.

I'll never tell you!

FOOD AND DRINK. The pirates will help themselves to your ship's supplies. The food and drink will fill their bellies, not yours.

NO FIGHTING. The captain does not allow fighting on board his ship. Any arguments will be settled by a duel on shore.

NO GAMBLING. The pirate crew are not allowed to bet money on card or dice games on board ship. They must save their gambling for the tavern.

13

No escape. Your new home

The pirates will keep you in the ship's hold. You will be locked in this dark, rat-infested place day and night, ankle deep in filthy, stinking bilge-water, stale air filling your lungs. You will lose all sense of time and soon you won't know how long you've been down there.

You can forget any thoughts you have of escape. You cannot climb out of the hold and even if you could you wouldn't get very far. The pirates have fitted heavy iron shackles to your legs, which make it hard for you to move around. You have to get used to this life!

Your new shipmates

QUARTERMASTER. He is the ship's second-in-command who loves using a cat-o'-nine-tails.

SURGEON. He's quick with a saw, so if you injure a limb he'll have it off in no time.

CARPENTER. He mends the ship's timbers and his skill with a saw means he can do surgeons' work too!

SAILMAKER. He makes and mends the ship's sails and other canvas items such as covers and awnings.

NAVIGATOR. Using measuring instruments like a backstaff, he plots a safe course for the ship to follow.

COOPER. He makes and repairs the ship's wooden barrels, which hold supplies of food and drink.

ORDINARY SEAMEN. They keep the ship in good order: swabbing the decks, manning the bilge pumps, working the sails, checking the rigging and so on.

Quartermaster

Carpenter

Surgeon

Navigator

Cooper

Sailmaker

Seaman

Comfortable? Good, 'cause you'll be there a while yet!

Handy hint

Give your fine coat to the ship's boy. He might remember this and help you when the time comes.

In irons! Shackled to the deck

A week of suffering

When the pirates eventually bring you up on deck, it's not because they're feeling sorry for you. Far from it – they are going to try and make you talk. To start with they'll clamp you in large, heavy leg irons called bilboes.

There you'll stay, fastened to the deck for seven whole days. You will feel the full force of nature – the cold wind, the lashing rain, the blistering sun and spray from the salty sea. Are you sure you don't want to tell the pirates where the rest of the fleet is?

Won't you help me, boy?

MONDAY. You're taken from the hold and put in bilboes.

TUESDAY. You've had nothing to eat or drink for a day and a night.

WEDNESDAY. You're very thirsty, but don't drink the saltwater you're offered.

THURSDAY. There was a storm last night and the huge waves and movement of the ship make you feel dizzy and seasick.

Your wig

Handy hint

Lick rainwater from your skin and suck it from your clothes – it's the only fresh water you'll get this week.

I can't! Cap'n would have me flogged!

Bilboes

FRIDAY. The sun beats down on your bald head all day so you get sunburnt.

SATURDAY. You're covered in blisters from the sun and salty wind and you're plagued by stinging, biting insects.

SUNDAY. You're thrown back into the hold with the rats and filthy water.

Flogged!

Cat-o'-nine-tails

THE CAT is nine lengths of rope, each about 60 cm long, tied to a wooden or rope handle. Each of the 'tails' has three knots tied in it, covered in tar to make them hard and sharp.

FISH HOOKS. Some quartermasters are known to tie fish hooks at the end of the cat's tails.

o far, so good – you haven't told the pirates where the rest of the treasure fleet is, which means you haven't betrayed your fellow seamen. But now the pirates decide the fastest way to loosen your tongue is with a good old-fashioned flogging by the quartermaster with the dreaded cat-o'-nine-tails.

Knots

MUSKETBALLS. Some cat-o'-nine-tails have lead musketballs fixed to the tails for extra stinging power.

SALT 'N' VINEGAR. After the flogging you might have salt and vinegar rubbed into your wounds. It stings!

NEW SHIRT. Your back will be cut to ribbons – seamen call this 'wearing a checked shirt'.

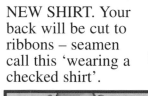

As the quartermaster lets the cat out of the bag where it is kept, you are spreadeagled and tied by your wrists to a grill on deck. The pirate captain decides how many lashes you'll receive – it could be forty, fifty, sixty, or more. At the end of it, he will ask you the same questions once again. Will you give in and tell him, or not?

Handy hint

If you're told to make the cat for your own flogging, tie one knot in each of its tails instead of three.

Groan

Twenty-six...

Vinegar

Salt

19

Keelhauled. Man overboard!

Water torture

THE PIRATES have many ingenious ways of using the sea to punish you.

DUCKING. You might be suspended from a yard-arm and ducked into the ocean while the ship sails along. Hold your breath!

TOWING. You might be tied to the end of a rope and tossed into the ocean, then towed along behind the ship for hours.

ou are incredibly brave! Despite everything the pirates have done, you haven't told them what they want to know. After the flogging they keep you in the ship's hold until the cuts on your back have healed – then they are ready for your next torture.

A rope is passed under the ship, from starboard to port. The pirates tie you to the rope and toss you overboard. You are about to be keelhauled – hauled by the rope, under the ship's keel. As your back scrapes along the ship's bottom, you'll be dragged over the razor-sharp barnacles that grow there. If you don't drown, you might die later from your wounds.

STITCHED UP. You might be sewn into a piece of old sailcloth with other prisoners and thrown overboard.

WEIGHED DOWN. You might be tied to a heavy weight, such as a dead body, then thrown overboard.

TARGET PRACTICE. You might become a target for the pirates to aim at. You'll just have to hope they're bad shots!

Fire! Burning and barrels

Feel the heat...

BURNING. Your arms and legs might be tied and pieces of burning rope stuffed between your fingers and toes.

The pirate ship has plenty of gunpowder on board but it is not just used to shoot cannonballs at other ships, as you will discover. Once again, the pirates drag you out of the hold and once again the captain demands to know where the treasure ships are. When you refuse to tell him, you are grabbed and bundled into a barrel filled with gunpowder. All it takes is one tiny spark to blast the barrel, and you, to smithereens! This could be your last chance to save your skin – before you lose it!

MORE THAN A MOUTHFUL. Pieces of oakum (unravelled rope) will be pushed into your mouth and then set alight.

BARBECUE. You might even be tied to a spit over the ship's cooking fire. You'll be roasted alive!

Diseased and done for

The gunpowder barrel is the last straw. The thought of being blown to bits is just too much so, as the fuse on the gunpowder is about to be lit, you break your silence. When you tell the pirate captain where the rest of the treasure ships are heading he decides to spare your pathetic life. Actually, he does it to save valuable gunpowder, but he wouldn't tell you that! Now you have to face up to a new danger: disease. You body is in poor condition and in your weakened state a deadly infection could set in. It would finish you off in no time at all.

I can't take any more!

Symptoms of sickness:

SCURVY. You will have pale skin, your teeth will fall out, your legs will swell up and you'll have terrible diarrhoea.

YELLOW FEVER. Mosquitoes carry this horrible disease. You will feel extremely hot for days, then you'll either get better, or vomit black blood and die.

DYSENTERY. This will give you awful pains in the stomach and non-stop diarrhoea.

24

Handy hint

If you get scurvy, eat lemons, limes or oranges to make you feel better. (They're full of vitamin C, but you wouldn't know that.)

GANGRENE. If this serious infection sets in to one of your wounds, the surrounding flesh will quickly die. The ship's surgeon (or carpenter) might decide to chop off an infected limb.

Don't worry! It's only a BIT rusty!

Marooned – alone forever?

On a deserted island

CANNIBALS. You should hope you won't meet any – you might end up in their cooking pots!

he pirates have the information they need. You're not worth anything to them now and the last thing they want is for you to catch a deadly disease and pass it on to the rest of the crew. They decide to get rid of you by leaving you stranded and alone on a deserted island. This is called marooning and you have become a poor unfortunate marooner. From now on you'll have to look after yourself, living off whatever you can find on the island – at least you've seen the last of the pirates! Perhaps, one day, the long arm of the law will catch up with them and they'll get what they deserve.

GO MAD. With no one to talk to, you might lose track of time and you could end up losing your mind.

STARVE. If there is no fresh water or food, it'll be the end of you within a few days.

RESCUE. Keep a look out for ships on the horizon. Light a fire to let them know you're here and hope they come to your aid.

Saved! The Navy to the rescue

What happens to the pirates?

At last you have had some luck! The day after you were marooned, a passing ship saw the smoke from your fire and came to your rescue. Your saviours were the crew of an English warship of the King's Navy, sent to track down the pirates who have been robbing ships.

HUNG BY THE NECK. Captured pirates will be 'turned off the cart' – hung until they're dead.

HUNG IN CHAINS. An executed pirate will be bound in iron hoops and left to swing until his bones are picked clean.

HEADS OFF. The heads of executed pirates will be displayed for all to see.

PARDONED. Those forced into piracy and who have never used weapons against others are pardoned and set free by the court.

Abandon ship!

28

You have valuable information for the Navy captain about those who captured you and he easily hunts the pirates down. The pirate sloop is no match for the guns of the warship. The pirate captain and all his crew are taken prisoner. Eventually, you take command of a new ship. But you will not get your treasure back – the Navy ends up with it!

Clean yourself up, buy some nice new clothes and a new wig, ready to begin life as the captain of a new ship.

Argh! That was close!

Glossary

Avast! A seaman's command to stop doing something.

Backstaff An instrument for measuring the height of the sun in the sky. It was used by a ship's navigator to work out the position of the ship.

Barnacle A shelled animal that attaches itself to rocks and wooden objects.

Bilboes A bar with sliding iron shackles fixed to the deck of a ship.

Bilge-water Seawater that collects in the hold of a ship.

Booty Treasure and valuables taken by pirates.

Cannibal An animal that kills and eats its own kind.

Cargo The goods carried in a ship or other vehicle.

Convoy A fleet of vessels that travel together for safety.

Cutlass A heavy sword with a slightly curved blade and a basket-shaped guard to protect the hand.

Flintlock pistol A pistol that fires when a gunflint (a piece of stone) makes a spark that ignites a small charge of gunpowder.

Friction The action of one object rubbing against another.

Galleon A large, slow-moving and heavily armed ship designed to carry cargo.

Haven A place of safety.

Hold The inside of a ship, where cargo is stored.

Jolly Roger The name of the flag flown by a pirate ship. Its name might have come from an old English word 'roger', meaning a beggar or the Devil, who was called 'Old Roger'.

Keel The timber that runs along the bottom of a ship and forms its backbone.

Musket A gun that fires a ball of lead.

New World A European name for North and South America.

Oakum A substance made from unravelled old rope. It was used to fill cracks in a ship's timbers.

Porcelain A white, hard, shell-like material like pottery, made of clay and rock.

Port The left side of a ship.

Prize A ship captured by pirates.

Rogue A dishonest or troublesome person.

Scurvy A disease caused by a lack of vitamins in the diet, particularly vitamin C.

Starboard The right side of a ship.

Yard-arm The end of a yard, which was the large beam to which a ship's sails were fixed.

Index